Contents

Characters

Robin Hood (real name: Robert Fitzooth)
Maid Marian

Will Scarlet Dickon Friar Tuck Little John Ed Harry Sam Thomas	outlaws

The Sheriff of Nottingham
Three of his men
The Sheriff's wife
Anna, barmaid at the Castle Hill Inn
Steve Bowman, the Sheriff's hangman
A beggar

Mrs Green Mrs Brown	at a market stall

Mrs Wood
Mrs Long
Two other women

5	**friar** ['fraɪə]	Bruder (Mönch)
14	**barmaid**	Bedienung im Gasthaus
14	**inn**	Gasthaus, Herberge
16	**beggar**	Bettler/in

Prologue

The curtain is still closed. Will Scarlet runs onto the stage, in front of the curtain. He is wearing a scarlet shirt, and carrying a bow.

Will: Hello, friends! Welcome! Welcome to Sherwood Forest! To the world of Robin Hood! – I think some of you know me already. I'm one of Robin's men. Maybe you even know my name. *(He points to his shirt.)* See what I'm wearing? See the colour? Yes, that's right – it's red. Scarlet! And that's my name, too: Scarlet. Will Scarlet.

You all know who Robin Hood is, I'm sure. An outlaw – yes, that's right. A man of the forest, a man without rights. But Robin Hood wasn't always an outlaw. Oh no! When I first knew him, he was a rich man, and he lived in a big house, Locksley Hall. His name wasn't Robin Hood in *those* days. It was Robert Fitzooth, and he was the Earl of Locksley Hall! And *I* was his servant!

	prologue ['prəʊlɒg]	Prolog, Vorspiel
1	**curtain** ['kɜ:tn]	Vorhang
2	**scarlet** [ɑ:]	scharlachrot, hochrot
8	**to point to**	zeigen auf
19	**earl** [ɜ:l]	Graf
20	**servant** ['--]	Diener/in

Maid Marian walks onto the stage, in front of the curtain.

Will: And this is Maid Marian, Robin Hood's sweetheart.

Marian: *(gives Will a hug)* Oh, Will! I hope I will be Robin's *bride* one day soon. (*to the audience*) – Yes, I'm Marian. Robin and I wanted to get married. That was when Robin was still an earl. But the Sheriff of Nottingham stopped the wedding! Yes! Think of it! The Sheriff and his men came to the church and *stopped our wedding!* In front of my father – and all our wedding guests!

Will: (*puts his arm round Marian's shoulder*) Don't worry, Marian! – You're always welcome at our camp in the forest.

Marian: I know that, Will. I come as often as I can. My father is against it, of course! (*angry now*) Just because Robin is an outlaw now! It was different when he was still an earl! Then my father liked him. But now? (*She gives Will a hug.*) I must go home now, Will! Give Robin my love when you go back to camp!

She runs off.

4	**sweetheart** ['swi:thɑ:t]	Schatz, Freund/-in
6	**bride** [braɪd]	Braut
6	**audience** ['ɔ:dɪəns]	Zuschauer, Publikum
7	**to get married**	heiraten
10	**wedding**	Hochzeit
16	**camp**	Lager
18	**against** [ə'genst]	gegen

Dickon runs onto the stage, in front of the curtain. He is carrying a small bow.

Will: *(to the audience)* And this is Dickon. He's the youngest in our camp. He came to us when his father died.

Dickon: (*to the audience*) It was so difficult for me and my father. We were so poor! One day my father shot a deer in the forest. The Sheriff's men caught him – and killed him! They left his dead body in the forest. (*He puts his hands over his face.)*

Will: So I took Dickon with me to Robin Hood. *(puts his arm round Dickon)* Now your home is with us, Dickon. – But these are terrible times! Our good King Richard is far, far away. He is fighting in the Holy Land.

Dickon: Long live King Richard!

Will: And now his brother, Prince John, is in charge of the country.

Dickon: Down with John!

Will: You're right, Dickon! John is a bad man, a cruel man. And most of his men are as bad as he is! He has put cruel sheriffs in our towns.

8 **deer (pl. deer)**	Rotwild, Reh
9 **to kill**	töten
16 **to fight** [aɪ]	kämpfen
16 **the Holy** ['həʊlɪ] **Land**	das Heilige Land
19 **in charge of** [tʃɑ:dʒ]	verantwortlich für
22 **cruel** ['krʊəl]	grausam

His tax collectors go from house to house and take as much money as they can. So poor people get poorer and poorer!

Dickon: Even rich people have no chance if they go against John and his men!

Will: That was what happened to my master, Robin Hood! He always helped the poor, and stood up for other people's rights. The Sheriff found out about it. Then he and his men took Robin's house – Locksley Hall. They took all his goods, too, and made him an outlaw!

Friar Tuck comes onto the stage, in front of the curtain.

Friar Tuck: Ah! Will! Dickon! There you are! Time to get back to camp. Come on!

Dickon: Why? Has anything happened, Friar Tuck?

Will: Nothing has happened, Dickon, you can be sure! The good Friar has come to tell us our meal is ready! Am I right, Friar?

Friar Tuck: Right first time, Will! One of Robin's old friends has brought us a goose! Roast goose! *(He puts his hands round his big stomach, closes his eyes, and smiles.)* And after that –

1 **tax collector** Zöllner
6 **master** Meister, Herr
11 **goods** Güter, Hab und Gut
19 **Right first time!** Gleich richtig geraten!

Will: OK, OK, Friar! Go back to camp and tell them we won't be long. (*to the audience*) And now, friends, it's time for some action! Come with us now – on one of our first adventures! It started one day when Robin heard news about his old family home – Locksley Hall. The Sheriff wanted to give Locksley Hall – as a present! – to one of his rich friends. So Robin sent me and Dickon – in secret, of course – to Locksley Hall, to find out what was happening ...

2	**We won't be long**	Wir sind gleich soweit, kommen gleich
10	**secret** ['si:krɪt]	Geheimnis, Geheim-
10	**in secret**	heimlich

Scene 1

The edge of Sherwood Forest. In the background we can just see Locksley Hall – like a small castle – behind the trees. In the foreground there are two or three small bushes, and on the left there is a hollow tree.
Will Scarlet and Dickon are crouching in front of one of the bushes. Will is wearing a brown jacket – perhaps with a hood – over his scarlet shirt.

Will: *(points to the Hall in the background)* There it is, Dickon! Locksley Hall! That's where I lived – as Robin's servant – not so very long ago. What do you think of it, Dickon? A fine house, eh?

Dickon: Fine? Wow! It's like a *castle*, Will – not just a house! It's almost as big as *Nottingham* Castle! It's fine enough for a king!

Will: All right then, Dickon. Now, this is our plan. Listen to what I tell you. I'll go into the house now. I can get in through the servants' door – at the back. *(He takes a big old key out of his pocket and shows it to Dickon.)* See? I've still got the key! You must wait for me here and –

1 **edge** [edʒ] Rand
1 **background** Hintergrund
3 **foreground** Vordergrund
4 **bush** [ʊ] Busch, Strauch
4 **hollow** hohl
5 **to crouch** [kraʊtʃ] kauern
21 **key** [kiː] Schlüssel

Dickon: Wait here? But Will! I want to come with you. I'll –

Will: No, Dickon. I must do this job alone. I know the house and you don't. I know every corner of it. The secret passages and –

Dickon: Secret passages! Oh Will! Can't I come, too? It sounds so exciting!

Will: *Too* exciting, probably. It'll be dangerous, Dickon. No, you'll be more useful if you stay here. – Wait for me, then. I'll be back as soon as I can.

He gets up and goes off through the trees.

Dickon: *(calls after him)* Good luck, Will!

Now Dickon is alone, and everything is quiet. Birds are singing in the trees. Dickon takes some bread out of his pocket, then he sits down in front of the bush and begins to eat. After a few moments he puts the rest of the bread away. He yawns.

Dickon: Good bread, that. I'll eat the rest later. – Well, I can't do much to help Will *here*. But he said: Wait – so I suppose that's what I must do. *(pause)* I think I'll just lie down for a minute or two. That can't be a mistake. *(He lies down.)* Ah! But just for a minute or two ...

5 **secret passage** ['pæsɪdʒ] Geheimgang
7 **to sound** [aʊ] sich anhören, klingen
18 **to yawn** [jɔ:n] gähnen
21 **I suppose** [sə'pəʊz] **I must** ich muss wohl, vermutlich

The lights go lower – to show that time is passing. There is a short pause. Bird song. Then – from back stage – the sound of voices, quiet at first, then louder. Three or four people are shouting, all at the same time.

Voices: Hey, who's that?/Who's that man?/What's he doing here?/Stop that man!/Who is it then?/Don't we know him?/After him, men!/Stop him!/He went that way!/Into the forest!/After him!

The lights come on full again. Suddenly Dickon wakes up. At the same moment Will Scarlet runs through the trees – to the bush where Dickon is. Will is carrying a bundle over his shoulder. At once he opens the bundle, takes out a small bag, and gives this bag to Dickon.

Will: Quick! Take this to Robin! (*He looks round in a hurry – to find a hiding place for Dickon. He sees the hollow tree on the left, and points to it.*) Hide in there! In you go! Quick!

1	**the lights** [aɪ] **go lower** ['ləʊə]	die Beleuchtung wird schwächer
1	**to pass** [ɑ:]	vergehen, vorbeigehen
13	**bundle** [ʌ]	Bündel
16	**in a hurry** ['hʌrɪ]	in Eile
16	**hiding place** ['haɪdɪŋ' pleɪs]	Versteck

Dickon jumps into the hollow tree, with the bag in his hand, and disappears. In a hurry, Will closes his bundle and throws it over his shoulder again. At that moment three of the Sheriff's men come through the trees. They block Will's way.

1st man: Stop! In the name of the Sheriff of Nottingham! Stop!

Will: Why, what's wrong? What do you want?

2nd man: What were you doing at Locksley Hall just now? We saw you when you were coming out. You've no right to go in and out of that house – and you know it! Who *are* you, anyway?

2 **to disappear** [ˌdɪsəˈpɪə] verschwinden
5 **to block s.o.'s way** jemandem den Weg versperren
12 **anyway** [ˈenɪweɪ] überhaupt, jedenfalls

Will: I was a servant at Locksley Hall when Robert Fitzooth still lived there. I came back to collect a few clothes, that's all.

3rd man: Let's see what's in that bundle, then! *(He pulls the bundle off Will's shoulder, opens it, and throws the things in it on the floor. He and the 1st man pick up some of the things and look at them.)* An old shirt! A shoe! A dirty sock! *(He holds it near his nose, then throws it on the floor.)* Ugh! *(to Will)* Don't you ever wash your socks, man?

1st man: Another shoe! A helmet! – Nothing wrong with that. Let him go, he's harmless enough.

Will: I'll put my things together again, then. *(He begins to pick things up.)*

2nd man: Hey, wait a minute! Don't I know that voice? *(He pulls Will towards him, then pulls his jacket open. Under it he sees Will's scarlet shirt.)* Scarlet! I thought so! It's Will Scarlet! I know the man! A traitor! One of Robin Hood's men!

Will: I'm not a traitor! I –

1st man Arrest him!

Will tries to run away through the trees, but the other two men catch him and bring him back. They hold his hands behind his back.

9 **to hold** [əʊ] halten
13 **harmless** harmlos
20 **traitor** [eɪ] Verräter
23 **to arrest** [-ˈ-] verhaften

1st man: *(to Will)* So you're Will Scarlet, eh? I think your name is on the Sheriff's list: "Wanted – Dead or Alive"! Did you know that? *(Will looks round, but he has no chance to escape.)* And do you know what happens to the outlaws on that list – when the Sheriff catches them? *(He puts his hand to his throat and makes a sign, and then a sound in his throat for 'dead'.)*

The other two men laugh.

2nd man: *(to Will)* It'll be the gallows for you tomorrow, Will Scarlet!

1st man: Off with him! Off to Nottingham Castle!

They take Will away.

Scene 2

Robin Hood's camp in Sherwood Forest. The outlaws are sitting together after a meal. Some are sitting on the floor, others on tree stumps. In the centre of the stage, Robin Hood and Maid Marian are sitting together. The outlaws (Sam, Thomas, Harry and Ed; Little John and Friar Tuck) are making music and singing. Robin and Marian are listening.

2 **Wanted – Dead** [ded] **or Alive** [ə'laɪv] Gesucht – tot oder lebendig
4 **chance** [tʃɑ:ns] Chance, Gelegenheit
5 **to escape** [ɪ'skeɪp] entkommen

Oh! Hear our song of Robin Hood
And drink with us in the forest green.
Our bows are strong and our arrows good
And our hearts are as merry as merry!

Long live Robin and Marian!
And long live Richard, our noble King!
We'll stay together as long as we live
And the birds in sweet Sherwood will sing.

Oh! Join our fight over hill and moor
Till we beat the Sheriff of Nottingham.
We stand for right and we help the poor
And our hearts are as merry as merry!

Long live Robin and Marian! *(chorus)*

Robin: *(claps and looks round at all the outlaws)* A merry song! Thank you, good friends! And now, dear Marian, would you like to sing us a song? Friar Tuck will play, I'm sure.

Marian: Of course I'll sing you a song! What about "Under the Greenwood Tree"?

3	**strong** [strɒŋ]	stark, kräftig
4	**heart** [hɑ:t]	Herz
4	**merry**	fröhlich
6	**noble** [əʊ]	edel, nobel
9	**moor** [ʊə]	Hochmoor
10	**till**	bis
10	**to beat** [i:]	schlagen

Note: You'll find the music for the song on page 44.

There are cheers from the outlaws. Just as Marian is getting ready to sing, Dickon runs onto the stage. He is out of breath – and very excited. At first he is too excited to speak.

Robin: Dickon! What happened? Where's Will? Isn't he with you? – Sit down, boy! – Thomas, give him a cup of wine.

Thomas gets a cup and Friar Tuck puts some wine in it.

Friar Tuck: This'll do the boy good. Wine makes the heart merry, as the Good Book says!

Dickon: *(takes the cup, but doesn't sit down)* They've caught Will! They've taken him to Nottingham Castle! They –

Outlaws: *(in dismay)* What?/Oh no!/Caught Will?/ This is terrible?/That's bad!/Taken him to Nottingham?

Robin: Quiet a moment! – Now, Dickon, tell us what happened – from beginning to end. Take your time. Well – did Will go into Locksley Hall?

Dickon: Yes, he went inside. I wanted to go with him, but Will said no. I waited for him at the edge of the forest. When he came back, he gave me this little bag – for you, Robin! (*He takes the small bag out of his pocket, and gives it to Robin.*)

1	**cheer** [ɪe]	Hurraruf, Jubel
3	**out of breath** [breθ]	außer Atem
7	**cup** [ʌ]	*hier:* Becher
14	**in dismay** [dɪs'meɪ]	empört

Little John: What's inside? Open it, Robin!

Robin opens the bag and takes out what is inside: jewels! He holds them up – and the outlaws gasp.

Harry: Jewels! Where do they come from?

Marian: Oh Robin! Aren't those your mother's jewels?

Robin: Yes, they're my family jewels. My mother wore them – and my grandmother, too, I remember. They're very old. Well done, Dickon! It's good that *these* didn't fall into the Sheriff's hands!

Dickon: But poor Will did! Oh, Robin, it was terrible! I hid in a hollow tree – with the little bag in my hand! I was so scared! I couldn't see what happened to Will – but I *heard* it all.

Robin: Did the Sheriff's men see Will – and follow him?

Dickon: Yes, he knew they were after him. – He had no chance. They arrested him and took him away with them. To Nottingham Castle, they said.

Marian: Poor Will!

Robin: Did they say anything else?

Dickon: Yes, they did. It'll be the gallows for Will. Tomorrow! That's what they said – the gallows!

Little John: The gallows? Never! We'll stop them! We'll all go to Nottingham!

3 **jewels** ['dʒuːəlz]	Juwelen
3 **to gasp**	(vor Staunen) nach Luft schnappen
15 **to follow** ['--]	folgen, verfolgen

Ed: We'll go to the castle!

Harry: We'll fight the Sheriff!

Thomas: And his men!

Sam: They won't get away with *this*!

Harry: We'll hang the Sheriff on his own gallows!

Ed: Hang the Sheriff? Now *that's* an idea!

Thomas: Great!

Sam: Fantastic!

Robin: Not so fast, friends! Not so fast! We must think of a plan. Will is a prisoner. But we can't rescue him from Nottingham Castle. The castle is too strong for that. No, we must think of some other way. Wait. Let me think. – Hm, does anybody know who the hangman is?

Harry: It's a man from Yorkshire. Steve Bowman is his name. He started work last month, I heard. Nobody wanted the job, but the money's good, so ...

Friar Tuck: Steve Bowman, you say? I know the man! He was at Fountains Abbey with me! But he didn't stay long. Drank too much, that was *his* trouble! So, of course –

Robin: You know him, Friar Tuck? Good! I have an idea ...

Robin goes to Friar Tuck and takes him to one side. He starts to talk to him in a low voice. Friar Tuck nods, and starts to smile.

4 **to get away with s.th** — ungestraft davonkommen
21 **Fountains Abbey** ['faʊntɪnz 'æbɪ] — Kloster in Yorkshire

Thomas: Do you want to go to Nottingham right away, Robin?

Robin: Not quite yet, Thomas. We'll go early tomorrow morning, I think.

Little John: Right, everybody, let's get ready. There's work to do here. You all know your jobs. – Put the wine away, Thomas! We want to be fit for tomorrow!

Thomas: Don't look at *me* like that, Little John! *I* never drink more than is good for me.

Ed: But Friar Tuck, eh? – Did you hear what Little John said, Friar? No more wine for you today!

Robin: *(gives Friar Tuck a friendly punch)* I'm not so sure about *that*, dear Friar! Are *you*? I think you'll have quite a bit of wine this evening. If our little plan goes right!

Friar Tuck: *(laughs)* I'm sure it will, Robin! Yes – I think I'll have a very merry evening! *(He waves and goes off.)*

Sam: Where's he going, Robin?

Robin: To Nottingham.

The other outlaws: Now? Come on then!/Let's go!/To Nottingham!/Nottingham, here we come!

Robin: *(puts up his hand)* No! Wait! We must stay here. It'll be our turn tomorrow.

14 **punch** [pʌnʃ] Schlag mit der Faust
19 **to wave** [eɪ] winken

Scene 3

Nottingham Castle. The Sheriff and his wife are having their evening meal. The Sheriff is sitting at one end of a long table, his wife at the other. There are candles on the table and a bottle of wine. They are having soup. The Sheriff is making slurping noises as he eats his soup.

Wife:	Archibald! *(The slurping noises go on.)* Archibald!! Please stop it now.
Sheriff:	*(looks up from his plate of soup)* Stop what?
Wife:	Stop what! You *know* what, Archibald! You're doing it again!
Sheriff:	Doing what?

5 **to slurp** [slɜ:rp] schlurfen

Wife: Making those terrible noises with your soup. Slurp! Slurp! And *you* the most important man in Nottingham? Ha! I bet even the outlaws in Sherwood Forest have better manners than *you*! What will Prince John think when he comes to Nottingham next week?

Sheriff: *(laughs)* Pah! Prince John will have other things to think about when he comes here. *(He goes on with his soup.)*

There is a knock at the door.

Sheriff: Come in!

One of his men comes in.

Sheriff: *(looks up from his soup)* Well, what is it, man?

Man: Excuse me, Master Sheriff – but we've caught one of Robin Hood's men. Will Scarlet!

Sheriff: *(puts his soup spoon down)* Will Scarlet, eh? Good! Good! So you aren't as stupid as I thought. – Well, where is he then?

Man: Downstairs, Master Sheriff. In the hall.

Sheriff: Downstairs in the hall? The dungeon is the place for traitors like him! Take him to the dungeon. Let him sleep there tonight – with the rats!

Man: Yes, Master Sheriff.

3	**to bet**	wetten
4	**manners**	Manieren
10	**there is a knock** [nɒk]	es klopft
15	**master**	*hier:* alte Form der höflichen Anrede
21	**dungeon** ['dʌndʒən]	Kerker

Sheriff: And tell him we'll hang him in the market square tomorrow. *(He laughs.)* As a warning to his friends in Sherwood Forest – Robin Hood and all the rest of them!

Man: Yes, Master Sheriff. *(He goes out.)*

Wife: What a bully you are, Archibald. A bully – and a coward!

Sheriff: Why? What do you mean, woman?

Wife: You send that poor outlaw to sleep with the rats. But *you* – you're scared if you just see a *mouse*! You –

Sheriff: *(looks away)* Quiet, woman! Or I'll put you in the dungeon, too!

Wife: Ha! You won't do that to *me*, "Master Sheriff"!

Scene 4

The Castle Hill Inn in Nottingham. Friar Tuck comes in and sits down at a small table with two chairs.

Friar Tuck: Hello! Is there anybody there?

Anna, the barmaid, comes in. She goes to Friar Tuck's table.

Anna: Good evening, Friar. And what can I get for you?

7 **coward** ['kaʊəd] Feigling

Friar Tuck: I'll have a plate of chicken soup. Bread with it, please. And a bottle of your best red wine! – I'm your first customer this evening, eh?

Anna: You are, Friar! It's still quite early, of course. – You're a stranger here in Nottingham, I think?

Friar Tuck: Yes, I'm just passing through. Nice place, Nottingham.

Anna: Well ... You'll be on your way again tomorrow morning, then?

Friar Tuck: Oh yes, I won't be in Nottingham long.

Anna: Then you'll miss the execution tomorrow.

Friar Tuck: Execution?

Anna: Yes, the Sheriff's men have caught one of the Sherwood outlaws. A dangerous man, they say. He goes to the gallows tomorrow. In the market square.

Friar Tuck: Oh dear, oh dear. I'm sorry to hear that! *(He shakes his head.)*

Anna: We get all the news right away here – so near the Castle, you see. The Sheriff's men are often in here in the evenings. His hangman is one of our regular customers.

Friar Tuck: Is he now?

Anna: Well, I must get you your chicken soup! *(She goes out. In a moment she comes back with a bottle and a cup.)* – Here's your wine, Friar! The soup will soon be ready.

3	**customer** ['---]	Kunde/Kundin
5	**you're a stranger** ['streɪndʒə] **here**	Sie sind hier fremd
7	**I'm passing through**	ich bin auf der Durchreise
12	**execution** [ˌeksɪ'kjuːʃn]	Hinrichtung
19	**to shake,** [eɪ] **shook, shaken**	schütteln

Friar Tuck: Thank you. *(He tastes the wine.)* Ah! Very good!

Anna goes out. A moment later Steve Bowman, the hangman, comes in. At first he doesn't look at Friar Tuck, but goes towards the next table.

Friar Tuck: Good evening to you!

Steve: Evening. *(He looks at Friar Tuck and stops.)* Why! It's Friar Tuck! *(He goes to Friar Tuck's table and shakes his hand.)* Good to see you, Tuck! And what are you doing here in Nottingham? – You remember me, don't you?

Friar Tuck: Now, wait a minute ... Why, yes, of course, that's it! You were at Fountains Abbey with me! Friar Steven!

Steve: That's right! Friar Steven I was *then*. *(He sits down at Friar Tuck's table.)* I left the Abbey a few years ago. Maybe you remember that, Tuck. Well – and I left the Church, too.

Friar Tuck: I'm sorry to hear that, Steven. – Well, I hope you have found good work outside the Church.

Steve: Well ... I –

Anna comes in with the soup and bread.

Anna: Good evening, Master Bowman. What can I get for you?

Friar Tuck:	Bring another bottle of your best wine, please! And another cup – for Master Bowman here. Wine makes the heart merry, as the Good Book says!

Anna goes out, then comes back with another bottle and cup. Friar Tuck pours wine into the cups. He picks up his cup.

Steve:	Thank you, Tuck. Well, nice to meet you here! This seems to be my lucky day!
Friar Tuck:	My lucky day, too, Steven! – Well, let's drink to old times, eh?

Steve: *(picks up his cup)* To old times!

They empty their cups. Friar Tuck picks up the bottle again, and pours more wine. They pick up their cups again and laugh.

6 **to pour** [ɔ:] gießen, einschenken

Scene 5

Sherwood Forest: on the way to Nottingham. A signpost (Nottingham: 3 miles) points to the right.

Robin Hood, Little John, Dickon, Ed, Harry, Sam and Thomas are all wearing cloaks over their green clothes. They are carrying their bows. Robin is just talking to the outlaws when an old beggar in a long black cloak with a hood comes through the trees from the right. He walks with a stick, and takes very slow steps.

Robin: Right, men! You all know what you must do. When we get near Nottingham, hide your bows under your cloaks. We'll go straight to the market square and –

Little John: Shh! Someone is coming, Robin!

Robin: *(to the beggar)* Good morning, friend. You're coming from Nottingham, I think?

Beggar: That's right. I'm on my way back home. There are crowds of people in the town today. I'm glad I've got away – I can't stand crowds!

Robin: Why? What's happening in Nottingham today? Is it market day? Or the Sheriff's birthday maybe?

1 **signpost** ['saɪnpəʊst] Wegweiser
4 **cloak** [əʊ] Umhang
6 **beggar** ['--] Bettler
8 **stick** Stock

Beggar: *(laughs)* Ha! Nobody will ever come to sing "Happy birthday" to the *Sheriff*, you can be sure of *that*! On his last birthday, when he was riding through the streets in his carriage, someone threw bad eggs at him – so I heard. Hit him, too!

The outlaws laugh.

Thomas: Great!

Sam: Fantastic!

Beggar: But there won't be much to laugh about today. No, the crowds have come for the execution.

Little John: Execution?

Beggar: Haven't you heard the news? The Sheriff has caught one of Robin Hood's men. Will Scarlet. They plan to hang him in the market square at twelve o'clock. It's bad news, very bad. Robin Hood and his men are great people. They do so much to help the poor. Nobody else does a thing!

Robin: Listen a moment, friend. I like your long black cloak. Can I buy it from you?

Beggar: Buy it? This terrible old thing? You can have it for five pence.

Robin: Thanks!

The beggar takes off his cloak and gives it to Robin.

Beggar: There you are. It's a bit dirty – but it's warm.

4 **carriage** ['kærɪdʒ] Kutsche

Robin puts it on and pulls the hood over his head. He takes a purse out of his pocket and takes out a handful of silver pieces. He gives them to the beggar.

Robin: Here you are, friend. – For you and your family. *(He makes a signal to his men, and they walk on – towards Nottingham.)*

Beggar: *(looks at the money in his hand, and counts it in great surprise)* Eight – nine – ten – twelve – Wait! You've given me too much! Wait! – I ...

3 **silver** ['sɪlvə] Silber

Note: In those days there were 240 pence (pennies) in a pound. A pound (240 silver pieces) was a lot of money.

Robin and the outlaws have disappeared.

Beggar: They've gone ! And I didn't even have time to say thank you. *(He starts to count again.)* Twelve – fourteen – sixteen – seventeen. Seventeen new silver pence! I could buy three new cloaks with this! *(He looks up, with his head on one side.)* But who was it? That's the question ... *(Pause. Then he hits his head with his hand.)* Robin Hood, of course! *Must* be! What an old idiot I am! *(He laughs.)* Well! Won't they be surprised at home when they hear I've met Robin Hood! And when they see *these*!

He looks at the money in his hand again. Then he puts it in his pocket, laughs again, and walks off. His steps are still slow, but his head is higher now.

Beggar: Robin Hood! Long live Robin Hood!

Scene 6

The market square. At the back of the stage there is a platform with the gallows on it. At the front, on the left, there is a market stall, with fruit and vegetables. Two women, Mrs Green and Mrs Brown, are standing behind the stall. They are serving two customers with baskets

10 **idiot** ['ɪdɪət] Dummkopf, Idiot((nur Phonetik?))
19 **platform** ['--] Plattform, Podest
22 **to serve** [ɜ:] bedienen

(Mrs Wood and Mrs Long). Two other women with baskets are standing on the right and talking.

Mrs Green: Who's next? Mrs Wood? – Yes, please?

Mrs Wood: A pound of those apples – and a nice big cabbage, please. That'll be all for today, Mrs Green. *(She gives Mrs Green her basket.)*

Mrs Green: Thank you. *(She puts the apples and cabbage in the basket.)* That's three farthings then, please, Mrs Wood.

Mrs Wood: *(gives Mrs Green the money)* Here you are. – It's lucky I've still got a few farthings in my purse. The Sheriff's men were in our village again yesterday. Collecting taxes. As usual!

Mrs Long: They were in *our* village, too. Tax collectors the Sheriff calls them. Thieves – that's what *I* call them! They go into people's houses and take what they see! They looked in all our cupboards yesterday. Even under the beds!

Mrs Brown: Ah! You mustn't keep money under your bed, Mrs Long. They always look there first.

Mrs Long: Don't worry, they had no luck under *our* beds. Just a dead mouse – that was the only thing under there this time! I wanted to give it to the tax collectors – as a present for the

2	**basket** ['--]	Korb
8	**farthing** ['fɑ:ðɪŋ]	Kupfermünze *(Note: There were four farthings in a penny.)*
12	**village** ['vɪlɪdʒ]	Dorf
13	**as usual** ['ju:ʒʊəl]	wie gewöhnlich
19	**to keep** [i:]	halten

Sheriff – but I didn't dare! – No, we've got a good hiding place for *our* money, you can be sure!

Mrs Green: What do they do with all the money? That's what *I'd* like to know! There's no justice in England these days – with King Richard away so long.

Mrs Wood: You're right there, Mrs Green. That Prince John is a bad man – I've always said so. I –

Mrs Brown: Don't speak so loud! You never know who will hear what you say. One word against Prince John – and they'll call you a traitor. And *that* means the gallows! *(She nods her head towards the platform.)*

Mrs Long: Poor old Will Scarlet will be the next!

Mrs Green: Do you know him?

Mrs Long: He lived in our village when he was a boy. When he was twelve or thirteen, he started work at Locksley Hall. That's not far from us.

While she is speaking, the outlaws (as in Scene 5) come on the stage from the right. Behind them Robin Hood, in the old beggar's cloak with the hood over his head, comes towards the centre of the stage. He walks like an old man.

Robin: *(in a different voice, like an old man)* Where's the prisoner, then? Haven't they brought him yet?

1 **to dare** [eə] wagen
5 **justice** ['dʒʌstɪs] Gerechtigkeit

Mrs Green: Not yet, Grandpa! Why? Are you in a hurry to see an honest man go to the gallows? Shame on you!

Robin: Yahh! A traitor, that's what *he* is ! A traitor!

Mrs Long: What do *you* know about it? Will Scarlet was never a traitor. He's an honest man – honest and good.

Robin: Honest? He's one of Robin Hood's men. A band of thieves, that's what *they* are! A band of thieves!

Mrs Green: They've brought more good to the poor people of Nottingham than our Sheriff ever has!

Mrs Brown: Watch what you say, Mrs Green. Not so loud!

Mrs Green: I don't like the Sheriff – and I don't care who knows it!

Outlaws: Shh! They're coming!/The Sheriff's men!/ They're here!

There is the sound of a trumpet, and a voice calls:

Stand back! In the name of the Sheriff of Nottingham! Stand back!

Three of the Sheriff's men come onto the stage, at the back. They bring Will Scarlet with them. His hands are behind his back, with rope round them. A murmur goes through the crowd. The Sheriff's men take Will onto the platform and put him under the gallows.

2 **honest** ['ɒnɪst]	ehrlich, anständig
3 **Shame** [eɪ] **on you!**	Du solltest dich schämen!
15 **I don't care**	es ist mir egal
24 **rope**	Seil, Strick
24 **murmur** ['mɜːmə]	Murmeln, Murren, Unmutsäußerung

The sound of a trumpet comes again, and a voice calls: The Sheriff of Nottingham!

The Sheriff comes onto the platform and stands at the side.

Sheriff: People of Nottingham! You see here, in front of you, a traitor and an outlaw! As you all know, there are dangerous men in Sherwood Forest – Robin Hood and his band! This man here is one of them! These outlaws rob honest people. They stop their carriages on the Nottingham road. Then they take their money! The road through Sherwood Forest is not safe for travellers now. This must stop! Today the first of Robin Hood's men will die at the gallows. The others will soon follow – I'll see to that! *(to Will)* William Scarlet! You are an outlaw and a traitor. In the name of the law of England, you must die at the gallows. As a warning to all other outlaws, your dead body will hang here in the market square of Nottingham until the end of this month!

There is a murmur from the crowd.

Sheriff: *(looks round)* Where's the hangman? *(to his men)* Well, where is he, then?

1st man: I – I don't know, Master Sheriff.

9 **to rob** berauben
18 **law** [ɔː] Gesetz

Sheriff: You don't *know*? What do you mean? It's your *job* to know, man! We need a hangman! – Well, doesn't anybody know where he is?

1st woman: *(from crowd)* Steve Bowman? He drank too much last night!

People in the crowd laugh.

2nd woman: *(from crowd)* Drank too much? No wonder – with a job like that!

Sheriff: *(angry)* This is no joke! We need a hangman, I tell you! If the idiot isn't here, someone else must do the job!

There is a murmur from the crowd.

Mrs Green: *(in a low voice)* He must be crazy!

Sheriff: Well, who wants to to do it, then? – For twenty pence? *(Nobody answers.)* – For thirty pence?

Everybody is very quiet. Then suddenly Robin, in the beggar's cloak, goes towards the platform.

Robin: *(as beggar)* I'll do the job for you! I'll hang him! But give me the thirty pence first!

1st woman: *(from crowd)* The old devil!

There are cries and shouts from the crowd. As Robin goes up to the platform, some of the crowd try to hold him back, but they can't stop him.

7 **No wonder!** ['wʌndə] Kein Wunder!
21 **devil** ['devl] Teufel

Sheriff: Stand back, everyone! Let him through! – Come here, my good man. Well, are you sure you can do the job?

Robin: I've seen lots of executions in my time, Master Sheriff! I can do the job. Easy!

Sheriff: All right then. – Well, what are you waiting for, man?

Robin: My thirty pence, Master Sheriff! *That's* what I'm waiting for. *First* you give me the money, *then* I do the job. That's the way I work, Master Sheriff. No other way!

Sheriff: *(angry, but tries not to show it)* Well – all right then. Here you are. *(He takes some silver pieces out of his pocket and gives them to Robin. There are jeers from the crowd.)*

Robin puts the money in his pocket, then he goes to Will Scarlet. He looks up at the gallows, then he whispers something in Will's ear.

Sheriff: What are you doing there, man? Are you talking to the prisoner?

Robin: Only a few words, Master Sheriff. I thought – maybe the prisoner has a last request.

Sheriff: Last request? Pah! There's no time for that now, man. We're late with the execution already. Come on now, do the job!

15 **jeer** [dʒɪə] Buhruf, Hohngelächter
18 **to whisper** [ˈwɪspə] flüstern

Robin goes behind Will and – with his back to the Sheriff – unties the rope round Will's hands.

Sheriff: *Now* what's happening? Can't you hurry a bit, man? I haven't got all day!

Robin: I'm just making the rope tighter, Master Sheriff!

Suddenly Robin throws off his cloak, and he and Will Scarlet jump down from the platform. In a moment Will runs into the crowd and Robin turns towards the Sheriff and draws his bow. While all this is happening, the Sheriff and his men step back in surprise.

Sheriff: What's this? – Help! It's a trick!

People from the crowd: It's Robin Hood!/It's Robin of Sherwood!/Look, it's Robin!/Robin Hood!

At the same time, the outlaws in the crowd throw off their cloaks and draw their bows.

Sheriff: *(to his men)* Don't just stand there! Stop them!

1st man: But how? Look how many there are!

Sheriff: Stop them, I say!

His men start to go towards the front of the platform. But they stop when they see that Robin and the outlaws have their bows ready. When they shoot, the Sheriff and his men hold up their arms in front of their faces.

2 **to untie** [ˌʌnˈtaɪ] losbinden, aufbinden, lösen
5 **tight** [aɪ] fest (angezogen), eng
10 **to draw** [ɔː] *hier:* spannen

Robin: Be careful, Sheriff! – Maybe we'll hit you next time! (*he laughs*) – Draw your bows again, men!

When Robin and the outlaws draw their bows again, the Sheriff gives a signal to his men and they run off, with their arms in front of their faces.

Sheriff. Quick! Back to the castle, men!

The outlaws and the others in the crowd laugh and point at them in fun.

Robin: Come on, men! Back to the forest! *(He takes the Sheriff's silver pieces out of his pocket and throws them to the people in the crowd.)* A present from the Sheriff! Here you are! Here! Take them! They're for you!

Robin and the outlaws wave, and run off together. The others run to pick up the silver pieces.

Mrs Green: *(calls after Robin)* God bless you, Robin!
The others: Long live Robin Hood!/Robin Hood for ever!/Robin Hood!/Hurray!

Scene 7

Robin Hood's camp in Sherwood Forest. As in Scene 2, the outlaws are sitting together. They are making music and singing. Will Scarlet is in the middle, with Robin and Marian. Only Friar Tuck is missing.

Oh! Hear our song of Robin Hood
And drink with us in the forest green.
Our bows are strong and our arrows good
And our hearts are as merry as merry!

Long live Robin and Marian! *(chorus)*

Near the end of the song, Friar Tuck comes through the trees. His steps are not very steady.

Little John: It's Friar Tuck!
Robin: Welcome, dear Friar! Come and sit down! Join us in our merry song! Look, we have Will with us again!
Friar Tuck: *(goes to Will and gives him a hug)* Will! My dear friend, I'm so glad!

3 **God bless you!** Gott segne dich!
9 **to be missing** fehlen
16 **steady** [e] fest, sicher

Little John: Thomas! Give the good Friar a cup of wine!

Thomas gets up and wants to get the wine, but Friar Tuck stops him.

Friar Tuck: No wine! No wine! Thank you, Thomas, but *no* wine for me.

Ed: No wine? *(To the others)* He must be ill!

They all laugh.

Friar Tuck: I *am* ill! – Well, no, not quite. But I had enough wine last night to make my heart merry for a very long time!

Robin: And your old friend Steve Bowman?

Friar Tuck: My old friend Steve had even more than I did! A long night we had together, Steve and I. When the time for the execution came, he was still asleep under the trees by the river!

Robin: That was a good place for him today! A *very* good place! – Well done, dear Friar. You did a good job there!

Thomas: Great!

Sam: Fantastic!

All the outlaws clap and cheer.

Marian: Now sit down, Friar Tuck, and join us in our music!

Friar Tuck sits down, so that he is on one side of Marian, and Robin Hood on the other. The music starts again.

15 **to be asleep** [-ˈ-] schlafen

Epilogue

Will Scarlet: And now it's time to say goodbye. But don't forget! If you are ever in Nottingham, come to Sherwood Forest and visit us! Our camp is deep, deep in the Forest, of course, so it isn't easy to find ... But maybe you'll be lucky. I hope so! – Till then, goodbye!

(He waves and runs off.)

epilogue ['epɪlɒg] Epilog, Nachwort
4 **deep** [iː] tief

Acting the play: Some tips

The Prologue: This part of the play explains the background, and helps to answer the questions: Who was Robin Hood? And why were there so many outlaws in those days? You can shorten the Prologue, of course – or you can leave it out and start with Scene I. (If you do this, maybe you could write "Programme Notes" – to give your audience an idea of the background.)

Scenery and props

- For the forest scenes, perhaps you could use big houseplants as bushes. Tree stumps – as "chairs" for the outlaws – are easy to get. If you can't "make" a hollow tree for Scene I, Dickon could hide behind a big bush. A green curtain could make a good backcloth.
- Try to get two big old chairs and an old table for the scene in Nottingham Castle. Remember: things like cups, bottles, candles. etc. must "look old" – like in the Middle Ages!
- Making a stall for the market scene will be easy. If the gallows are difficult to make, perhaps you can just hang up a piece of rope.

- Bows are easy to make. Don't use arrows, of course! The outlaws can just "pretend" to shoot when they draw their bows.

8	**scenery** ['si:nərɪ]	Bühnendekoration, Kulissen
8	**props**	Requisiten
9	**houseplants**	Zimmerpflanzen
17	**the Middle Ages** ['mɪdl 'eɪdʒəs]	das Mittelalter
22	**to pretend** [prɪ'tend]	so tun als ob

Clothes: Try to find green shirts and green or brown tights for Robin and his men. (Only Will Scarlet wears a red shirt.) Friar Tuck is a monk, so try to find the "right" clothes for him (brown is the best colour); he must have a big stomach – so maybe you can use a pillow for this! A black shirt and black tights are probably best for the hangman.

Try to get helmets and make "swords" for the Sheriff's men. Maybe you can make a big gold "chain" for the Sheriff to wear.

Music: You can sing the outlaws' song to the tune of the famous "Greensleeves". (The music is on page 44.) Perhaps one (or more!) of the outlaws can play the guitar – or the recorder!

Characters: There are twenty-four characters in the play. If there aren't enough parts for everyone in your class, add more outlaws to Robin's band – or put more people in the crowd scene. Or if there are too many parts, some people could take more than one. (The hangman could also take the part of the beggar, for example. Or the Sheriff's wife could later be one of the Sheriff's men!)

Most important – Have fun!

8	**sword** [sɔ:d]	Schwert
9	**chain** [tʃeɪn]	Kette, Amtskette
11	**tune** [ju:n]	Melodie
14	**recorder** [-'--]	Blockflöte

The Robin Hood Song

Tune: Greensleeves, English traditional

Note: "B" (ll.2, 4, 6 and 8) is "H" in German!

Sherwood Forest activities

1. Let's play 'Hangman'

'Hangman' is very popular in Britain. You can play it with all the class, or in a group – or with just two players. First, player 1 (the 'hangman') thinks of a word (from the play!). He writes a blank (–) for each letter on the board (or on a piece of paper). Now the others try to find out what the word is. So they ask questions about the letters in it. If the answer is "yes", Player 1 must write that letter in. If it's "no", Player 1 starts to draw the 'gallows' (the picture shows you how). After ten "no's", the other players must 'go to the gallows' – and the 'hangman' wins the game. But if the other players find out what the word is, the 'hangman' *loses the game.

Example: Player 1 thinks of the word 'Sheriff' (7 letters):

___ ___ ___ ___ ___ ___ ___

Player 2: Is there a 'T' in it?
Player 1: No, there isn't.
Player 3: Is there an 'E' in it?
Player 1: Yes! The 3rd letter is 'E'.
Player 4: Is there an 'A' in it?
Player 1: No, there isn't.
Player 5: Is there an 'F' in it?
Player 1: Yes, you're lucky! There are two 'F's'. Look!

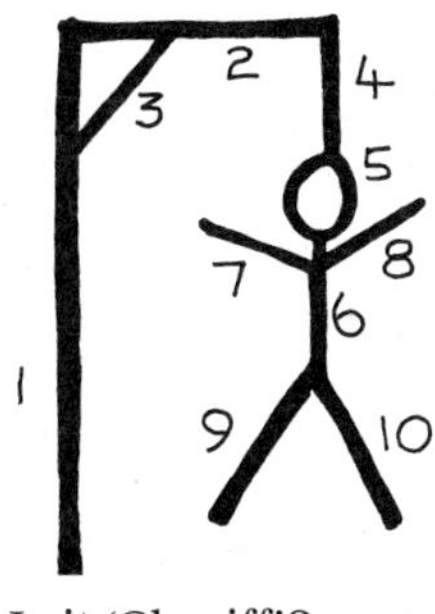

Player 2: I think I know the answer! Is it 'Sheriff'?
Player 1: Yes, it is! OK, you've won! Now it's your turn to be 'hangman'!

to lose [lu:z], **lost, lost** verlieren

2. I met Robin Hood ...

a) This is an alphabet game. It's easy to play. But you must remember what people 'had' in Robin Hood's time! The example will show you how it goes.

JULIA: I met Robin Hood – and he gave me an <u>A</u>PPLE.
MAX: I met Robin Hood – and he gave me a <u>B</u>OTTLE OF WINE.
LISA: I met Robin Hood – and he gave me a <u>C</u>AMERA.
FRANK: No, they didn't have cameras in those days!
LISA: OK ... a <u>C</u>ANDLE. Did they have candles?
ALEX: Yes, I think so. That's OK.

Can you go on? Use the Alphabetical Word List in your English book if you get stuck. (But try without it first!)

b) At the end, try to remember all the words. Take turns, or make a list. Can anyone remember them all?

3. I'll begin, then you go on

Tell your own Robin Hood story! Easy! One player says (or writes) a sentence. Then it's the next person's turn. Then the next. But remember: each player can only add ONE sentence! The example shows how you could start.

SOPHIE: One day Robin Hood and Little John went to Nottingham.
FELIX: On their way they met an old woman.
PAUL: "Please help me!" she said when she saw them.

(Don't forget! This game can be a lot of fun if you all 'work together'. Each player must be 'open' to all the other players' ideas. If you have a fantastic idea and then another player 'turns' the story with a different idea, try NOT to get angry!)

4. Your own Robin Hood game

Why not make your own *board game? You will need:

- two *counters – for two outlaws – and a dice;
- a big piece of paper (A3 is best);
- a big piece of card – for the board;
- a pencil, crayons – and lots of good ideas!

1. Think what 'background' or 'scene' you want for your game. Sherwood Forest? The town of Nottingham? The Nottingham road? Or all three together?
2. Draw the background scene on your paper. Where will the 'Start' be? And the 'Finish'? Put these in. Then draw the 'route' and put in the numbers ① to (55) from 'Start' to 'Finish'. Put interesting 'places' on your route – or places where it could be 'dangerous'.
3. What can happen on your adventure route? Collect 20 ideas (some 'good', some 'bad'), then write them in next to 20 of the numbers. Here are some examples:
   - Hide here from the Sheriff's men. *Miss one turn.
   - You've forgotten your bow and arrows. Go back to camp and start again.
   - Take a short cut through the trees to number ... .
   - A rich lady gives you a lift in her carriage. Go on to number ... .
   - You've helped an old man. Take an extra turn ...
4. Colour the game in, and *stick the paper on the card.
5. Wait until you throw a six – then you can start!

board game	Brettspiel
counter	Spielfigur
miss one turn	einmal aussetzen
to stick, stuck, stuck	kleben

5. A Robin Hood puzzle

1. Robin and his men saved Will Scarlet from the ...
2. People can get married in a ...
3. Steve Bowman once lived and worked at Fountains ... in Yorkshire.
4. 240 ... pieces were a pound in Robin Hood's time.
5. An ... was a man without rights.
6. You need a bow if you want to shoot with an ...
7. A ... is an enemy to his or her King and country.
8. The Sheriff's men killed Dickon's father and left his ... *(two words)* in the forest.
9. The most important man in Nottingham was, of course, the ...
10. Will was a prisoner in the ... at Nottingham Castle.
11. '... Tuck' really means 'Brother Tuck'.
12. "Will is a prisoner? We must go to Nottingham and ... him!"